THE COOLEST JOBS ON THE PLANET

Volcanologist

Hugh Tuffen with Melanie Waldron

Raintree

Chicago, Illinois

Edited by Andrew Farrow, Christine Peterson, and
Helen Cox Cannons
Designed by Cynthia Akiyoshi
Original illustrations © Capstone Global Library Limited 2014
Illustrated by HL Studios
Picture research by Mica Brancic and Tracy Cummins
Production by Helen McCreath
Originated by Capstone Global Library Limited
Printed and bound in China

18 17 16 15 14
10 9 8 7 6 5 4 3 2 1

Library of Congress Cataloging-in-Publication Data
Tuffen, Hugh, author.
  Volcanologist : the coolest jobs on the planet / Hugh Tuffen with
Melanie Waldron.
     pages cm. — (The coolest jobs on the planet)
  Includes bibliographical references and index.
  ISBN 978-1-4109-6643-8 (hb) — ISBN 978-1-4109-6649-0
(pb) 1. Tuffen, Hugh — Juvenile literature. 2. Volcanology — Vo-
cational guidance — Juvenile literature. 3. Volcanologists — Biog-
raphy — Juvenile literature. 4. Volcanoes — Juvenile literature. I.
Waldron, Melanie, author. II. Title.

QE34.T84 2015
551.21023 — dc23   2013040702

Acknowledgments
We would like to thank the following for permission to reproduce
photographs: Alamy pp. 14 (Pictures Colour Library/© Travel
Pictures), 17 (© Arctic Images/Ragnar Th Sigurdsson); C. Ian
Schipper p. 5; Getty Images pp. 4 (Perspectives/Carl Shaneff),
18 (DigitalGlobe), 37 (Christie Goodwin); Hugh Tuffen pp. 6, 7,
8, 9 bottom, 9 top, 11 bottom, 11 top, 12, 13, 19 bottom, 20,
21, 22, 23, 24, 25, 26, 27, 28, 29, 30, 31 bottom, 31 top,
32, 33, 34, 38. 39; Jeffrey A. Karson p. 36; Martin Rietze p. 15;
Mike R James pp. 40, 41; Rosanna Smith p. 35; Shutterstock pp.
19 top (sunsinger), 42 chair (OZaiachin), 42 clock (Jeff Lueders),
42 microscope (Prasolov Alexei), 42 middle rock (Apollofoto), 42
rocks (Viktoria), 43 backpack (Sergey A. Kravchenko), 43 books
(Quang Ho), 43 calculator (Artur Synenko), 43 hand (DenisNata).
Design elements Shutterstock.

Cover photo of a volcanologist standing over a volcano reproduced
with permission of Getty Images/National Geographic.

Every effort has been made to contact copyright holders of
material reproduced in this book. Any omissions will be rectified in
subsequent printings if notice is given to the publisher.

All the Internet addresses (URLs) given in this book were valid at
the time of going to press. However, due to the dynamic nature
of the Internet, some addresses may have changed, or sites may
have changed or ceased to exist since publication. While the author
and publisher regret any inconvenience this may cause readers, no
responsibility for any such changes can be accepted by either the
author or the publisher.

Contents

A Job with a Bang! 4

How I Became a Volcanologist 6

My First Big Research Project. 8

Exciting New Projects 10

Volcano Alert: Why
We Need Volcanologists 14

My Research on Volcanoes 18

Working on Volcanoes 24

A Day in the Field. 30

Volcanoes in the Lab 32

A Day in the Office. 38

How to Become a Volcanologist . . . 40

Quiz 42

Glossary 44

Find Out More 46

Index 48

A Job with a Bang!

Imagine standing on the sides of a volcano, watching as red-hot lava explodes out of its rim. The heat is incredible, the noise is terrifying, and the ground beneath you shakes as the volcano erupts. Now imagine that it is your job to be standing there! I am a volcanologist, and this is my job.

A volcanologist's job involves traveling all over the world to see eruptions and study volcanoes. Volcanologists have to collect samples of lava and rocks such as pumice to analyze in a laboratory. We also build computer models of erupting volcanoes.

Being a volcanologist is an exciting job.

This is me, working on Cordón Caulle, a volcano in Chile.

Did you know?

The 1883 eruption of Krakatoa in Indonesia was so loud that people heard it 2,891 miles (4,653 kilometers) away. It may have made the loudest sound in human history!

There are over 500 dangerous volcanoes around the world. As you are reading this, about 20 are erupting! Millions of people can be affected by volcanic eruptions. My job as a volcanologist is to help forecast when volcanoes are going to blow.

My job also involves studying what happens after a volcano has erupted. I look at the type of lava and ash that the volcano throws out. I help people to understand how the lava and ash will move and affect them. People working on volcanoes are specially trained to watch out for dangers and keep themselves safe.

How I Became a Volcanologist

My fascination with rocks—and volcanoes—started early. I grew up in the north of Cumbria, a county in the north of England. I loved to go walking and climbing on nearby hills. When I was a teenager, I was amazed to learn from a book that many of these hills were actually extinct volcanoes. I never realized that I had been walking over lava and ash for all these years. This first sparked my interest in volcanoes.

This is me as a 10-year-old on top of a hill in Cumbria with my dog, Liffey.

TOOLS OF THE TRADE: Volcanologists need to enjoy science! Physics and chemistry are especially important. It is also a good idea to study math. Some of my work involves working with data and presenting it correctly.

High school and college

In high school, I had some great science teachers. I got good grades and decided to continue studying science in college. Part of my studies involved studying an extinct volcano on the Scottish island of Arran. Standing inside this long-dead volcano, looking at the amazing rock formations, and thinking about the way they came about—I was hooked!

I got my degree in geology in 1997 and then decided to study for a master's degree in volcanology in France. I saw my first-ever volcanic eruption on Mount Etna in Italy. I will never forget watching from the crater edge as huge chunks of lava were blasted high into the sky above us.

This is me on vacation in Reykjavík, Iceland, after I completed my master's degree. Iceland is a place I have visited many times during my career.

My First Big Research Project

After I finished my master's degree, I decided to apply to Lancaster University, in England, to study for a PhD—a higher degree—in volcanology. I was really eager to study a mysterious volcano in Iceland called Torfajökull (pronounced TOR-vah-yo-kutl), shown here. It has produced some enormous eruptions, yet few people have studied it and no one has seen it erupt. I was thrilled to be offered the chance to study what had happened during some of its biggest eruptions, working alongside some top volcanologists.

NOTE TO SELF

It's important to take a tarp for camping on a volcano. It can be so useful: as a tent groundsheet; as a shelter from rain or falling ash; as a windbreak; or even as a sled for sliding down snowy slopes!

Now for the science...

The fieldwork was not just about having fun in amazing locations! We had to figure out some puzzling things about the volcano's eruptions. There were some exciting moments when we discovered some extraordinary cracks inside lava flows that nobody had ever described before. I remember getting goosebumps when I realized that these cracks could explain a long-standing mystery— exactly how earthquakes can be triggered inside volcanoes.

At the edge of a lava flow, there are natural hot pools to swim in. I made some great friends in Iceland and decided I had the best job in the world.

A hammer and chisel are used to take samples of lava.

Exciting New Projects

After my work on Torfajökull, I collected all my findings into a long report called a thesis. In 2002, I became Dr. Hugh Tuffen.

I spent some time back in Iceland helping scientists monitor some active volcanoes. Then I moved to Munich, Germany, to work with one of the world's best teams of volcano researchers. From there, I studied one of the most explosive volcanic eruptions ever—at Taupo in New Zealand.

This map shows the locations of places mentioned in this book. The black triangles are volcanoes.

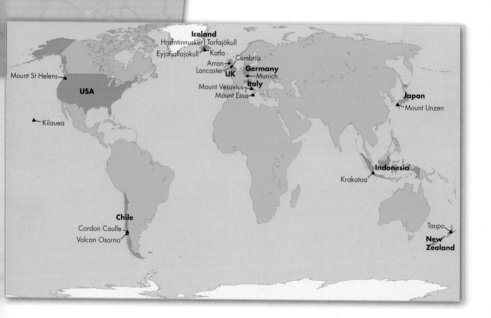

Testing my ideas

After studying Taupo, I returned to the United Kingdom to test an idea that I had. I heated up pieces of lava in the laboratory, then smashed them up. I used my results to figure out that when huge cracks form in lava inside volcanoes, earthquakes can be triggered. This discovery has helped volcanologists like me to understand what happens inside volcanoes before eruptions.

My hero!
Dave McGarvie (born 1957)

Dave McGarvie is a Scottish volcanologist who was my supervisor for my PhD. He is a fountain of knowledge on Icelandic volcanoes. He has taught me a great deal about fieldwork and eruptions under ice. He also gave me lots of great tips for camping on remote, snowy volcanoes. For example, he told me about cooking rice in a boiling mud pot (mud pool), and about organizing my days so that there's time for a great toboggan ride back to the campsite!

This is a piece of Icelandic lava after I smashed it to pieces in the lab (inset).

11

Red-hot lava is steaming away inside the crater of Mount St. Helens in 2006.

Working on Mount St. Helens

The next big volcano project I worked on was on Mount St. Helens, in Washington state, from 2006. This volcano had erupted in 1980, killing 57 people. We got the chance to fly over the top of the volcano's crater in a tiny airplane, in order to photograph the crater and the growing pile of lava.

During this trip, one of our camping sites was inside the crater of the volcano as it was erupting. This was really exciting, but definitely scary! I woke up in the middle of the night to hear the sound of rocks breaking. I jumped out of my tent, thinking a major explosion had started. But the noise was just a huge part of a cliff beneath our campsite that was collapsing.

Realizing I could help save lives

I visited Mount Unzen in Japan in 2007. The volcano was erupting between 1990 and 1995. When I was there, I saw how the volcanologists working there could help save lives. They were constantly measuring and monitoring the volcano. They were able to warn people to leave the area when they thought the volcano was becoming dangerous.

The heat of the pyroclastic flow on Mount Unzen melted and burned all the plastic, wood, and rubber from this fire engine, leaving just the bare metal.

Volcano Alert: Why We Need Volcanologists

Throughout history, there have been some huge, devastating volcanic eruptions, killing thousands of people. Part of the work that I do is to try to help protect people from volcanic eruptions.

Mount Vesuvius, Italy

A surprise eruption

Almost 2,000 years ago, near Naples, Italy, Mount Vesuvius erupted. A huge pyroclastic flow engulfed the whole area. Thousands of people were buried alive. Today, over four million people live nearby Mount Vesuvius—and it is likely to erupt again in the near future.

Volcanologists are using computer models to predict which areas are threatened by pyroclastic flows and lavas from Mount Vesuvius. They are also measuring earthquakes and gases at the volcano to detect any changes in its behavior.

Grounding air travel

In 2010, a volcano called Eyjafjallajökull (pronounced AY-yah-FYAH-dlah-YER-kutl) erupted in Iceland. A huge ash cloud drifted toward Europe. This led to enormous disruption to air travel around the world, as aircraft engines can be damaged by ash. Hundreds of thousands of flights were canceled, leaving many travelers stranded.

After the eruption of Eyjafjallajökull, many scientists became convinced that it was important to study Icelandic volcanoes.

Did you know?

The pyroclastic flow from Mount Vesuvius dumped up to 60 feet (18 meters) of ash and pumice on the people living in the Roman towns of Pompeii and Herculaneum. In the 19th century, archaeologists working on the sites found hollows in the ash. These showed where the bodies had lain before decaying away.

Hazardous volcanoes

Many of the world's volcanoes are closely monitored by volcanologists and other scientists. However, there are many volcanoes in places such as Indonesia and Latin America that are still not properly monitored. Different volcanoes are hazardous in different ways.

Some volcanoes release clouds of ash that sweep down their sides, destroying everything in their path. Other volcanoes send enormous ash plumes into the sky. Red-hot lava comes from many volcanoes, either as fast-flowing rivers or as thick mounds that gradually pour out of the mountain. Volcanoes can suddenly collapse, generating devastating rock avalanches and tsunamis. Ice-covered volcanoes are especially dangerous, as melting ice can trigger powerful, sudden floods.

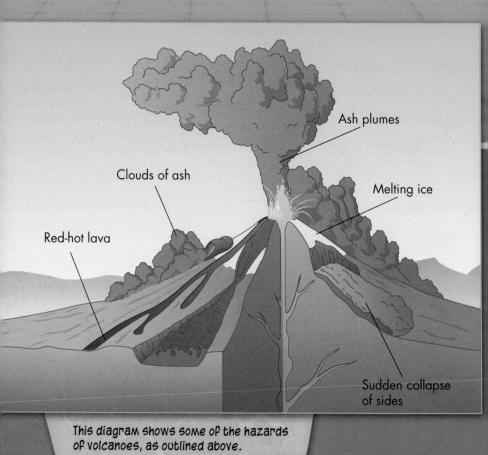

This diagram shows some of the hazards of volcanoes, as outlined above.

Volcanologists must have confidence in their instruments and be sure of their results. Telling people to evacuate when there is no real danger can be a problem, because the next time they are told to evacuate, they may decide to stay put instead. This time, however, the danger might be real.

Saving lives!

A volcanologist's job is to investigate how and why volcanoes erupt. Many volcanologists work on active volcanoes, and part of their job is to help forecast when a hazardous eruption is about to start. This gives people living near the volcano time to escape the danger. Saving lives in this way is an important part of a volcanologist's job.

Volcanoes give some signs that they are about to erupt. Sometimes the ground around the volcano swells. Sometimes there are earthquakes when rocks inside the volcano crack. Many volcanoes release toxic gases from their craters. Volcanologists monitor all these things.

Volcanologists in Iceland collect ash from the powerful explosive eruption of Eyjafjallajökull. They will then take it back to the lab and analyze the shape of the ash particles to see what drove the explosions.

My Research on Volcanoes

I am very interested in explosive eruptions, where magma is ripped to pieces in powerful explosions that can blast ash high into the sky. I want to research what happens inside a volcano before the explosive eruption happens.

Changing eruptions

I am also interested in how and why volcanic eruptions suddenly change. Some volcanoes switch from powerful explosive eruptions to more gentle eruptions, when lava slowly oozes out.

In this photo, Cordón Caulle in Chile is erupting explosively. The huge ash cloud creates thunderstorms with powerful lightning flashes.

This is Volcan Osorno, an ice-covered volcano in the south of Chile, which last erupted 150 years ago. Many people live in nearby towns and villages.

Fire under ice

My final area of research involves volcanoes that lie under huge caps of ice. When they erupt, they can trigger devastating floods as the ice suddenly melts. Very little is known about these dangerous volcanoes.

TOOLS OF THE TRADE: FIELD NOTEBOOK

Although volcanologists take more and more sophisticated equipment onto volcanoes, the most useful tool is always a field notebook. I use mine to sketch the eruptions and rocks I see, write down ideas, and record any measurements that I make. Sometimes bad weather means I'm stuck in my tent for days at a time. In this case, I can also use my notebook to keep a diary and write letters to friends and family. As soon as I get home, I photocopy my whole notebook, because I'm scared of losing it! On the right is a copy of a page from my notebook written during my fieldwork in Iceland.

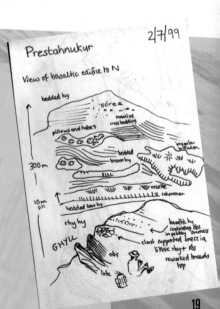

Studying Mount Etna

Mount Etna, in Italy, is one of the world's most active volcanoes. It erupts almost every year. I am studying what happens inside the lava as it flows down the volcano's sides. I take samples of the lava and "cook" it in the laboratory, until it is over 1,800 degrees Fahrenheit (about 1,000 degrees Celsius)! Then I can study how crystals grow inside the lava as it cools, as this thickens the lava and slows it down. The results will help us to predict how far away from the volcano people will need to be evacuated.

Mount Etna in Italy erupted explosively in April 2013.

An eruption in waiting

I am also working on Katla in Iceland. It is a huge volcano that is covered in ice. When it last erupted, in 1918, the ice melted extremely quickly. A huge torrent of water—more powerful than the Amazon River—poured down its sides. Many scientists are afraid that it will erupt again soon. It is such a massive volcano that an eruption could have terrible effects—much worse than at Eyjafjallajökull in 2010.

Volcanologist Jacqui Owen crosses a plain of black volcanic ash as she walks toward Katla.

Did you know?

The immense flood triggered by the 1918 Katla eruption is thought to have been up to 66 feet (20 meters) deep and moved at over 20 miles (32 kilometers) per hour. It carried enormous icebergs and boulders the size of houses. An ancient Icelandic legend says that a witch called Katla causes the eruptions, and that she possesses a magical pair of pants that allow people to run as far as they like without getting tired!

Help from other scientists

There is so much to understand about volcanoes! Many scientists help me in my research. Each one is an expert in his or her area, and they all help me to understand the different processes that are going on. Chemists help me to understand exactly what different lavas are made of and which gases come out of volcanoes. They can measure the different elements inside the lava—for example, copper and argon. Their information can help me to understand how lavas behave differently.

Tamsin Mather, a chemist and volcanologist, uses special equipment to monitor the gases coming out of volcanoes and measure their composition (what they are made of). Tamsin has found that volcanoes give off huge quantities of toxic metals such as mercury.

My hero! Magnús Tumi Guðmundsson (born 1961)

Magnús Tumi Guðmundsson is an Icelandic physicist and geologist who has made some real breakthroughs in understanding eruptions at ice-covered volcanoes. He found me a job monitoring Icelandic volcanoes after my PhD. He also lent me his best suit when I went straight from a volcano to an important meeting and only had dirty field gear to wear! We are still working together on Icelandic volcanoes.

Numbers and rocks

Physicists are scientists who use mathematics to explain how things move and change. They help me to understand what happens to lava when it cools down. I work with a physicist to model lava flows on computers. We can use these models to figure out where flows will go and how fast they will move.

Geologists are experts in understanding different rocks and their properties. I work with geologists who specialize in different areas. Yan Lavallee is a rock physicist and geologist who studies how volcanic rocks flow and break. In the picture below, he is using a permeameter while working in Japan. This is a machine that sucks air through lava to measure how easily gas can flow and escape.

Working on Volcanoes

During my fieldwork on volcanoes, I carry out many tasks, depending on the type of volcano I am working on and the research I am doing.

Ian Schipper and I stand at the foot of a lava flow in Chile, while blocks the size of tables tumble down. The lava makes extraordinary cracking noises that sound like thousands of plates being smashed.

Rivers of red rock

Volcanoes such as Mount Etna in Italy and Kilauea in Hawaii produce long rivers of lava. We can learn a lot from observing and collecting samples from lava flows. This can mean being close to red-hot lava—but not too close. I know people who have melted the soles of their boots by standing on lava that was too hot! However, not all lava is like a hot, red river—like the flow in the picture above.

Here, Harry Pinkerton is collecting a sample from an active lava flow on Etna. Protective clothing is essential because the heat is fierce.

NOTE TO SELF

We spend a lot of time thinking about safety and never take risks. We have plans in place in case the eruption suddenly changes, and we constantly monitor the volcanic activity. You should never work alone on an active volcano.

Taking lava samples

I collect samples of lava with either a hammer or a drill. Thick gloves might be needed if the lava is still hot. Samples are usually fist-sized lumps. I note where I collect each sample, using a GPS, then photograph and label it. After that, I put each sample in my backpack (which can get heavy at the end of the day) and carry them back to camp. At the end of a trip, I send the samples back to the United Kingdom in crates.

Collecting ash

It is really useful to collect samples of ash as it falls from a volcano, before it hits the ground or is mixed with rainwater. With this ash, you know exactly when it was blasted out of the ground, and all the chemicals in it are fresh. The ash cools as it falls and can be collected on paper or even brushed from our tents.

TOOLS OF THE TRADE: CAMERA

I always take a good camera on my fieldwork trips. It is very useful to film explosive eruptions. This is because you can then watch them over and over again, examining how often and how high the explosions appear and learning a lot about what controls them. We can even make 3D models of the shape of a lava flow using photographs!

Jon Castro and Ian Skilling watch the ash plume at Cordón Caulle in 2012, from a safe distance. We could see blocks of lava the size of cars being blasted into the air.

Staying out of harm's way

When I work on volcanoes that are erupting, I have to be very careful where I set up camp. It has to be on high ground, in a place where pyroclastic flows can't reach it and where dangerous volcanic gases can't gather. It has to be far enough from the crater that no large pieces of lava or pumice can fall on it. It also has to have a view of the crater, so that I can see if the volcanic activity suddenly increases.

Here I am camping under an ash plume at Cordón Caulle, Chile, in 2012. That morning we had awoken to find our tents covered in ash!

Ancient volcanoes

Detective work on ancient volcanoes can tell us all kinds of things about how volcanoes behave and what happens inside them. Eruptions in the past have created layers of lavas and ash that we can now safely study. We can figure out amazing things about what happened thousands or even millions of years ago in the world's biggest eruptions. It's like visiting a crime scene and trying to solve the puzzle of "whodunnit"!

The volcanologist Jacqui Owen stands on top of thick ash layers from a powerful eruption at Hrafntinnusker in Iceland.

This is a dike of lava in Iceland— it's a crack in the ground through which lava has risen upward. This is my favorite one, as it is where I first realized that the cracking of lava could trigger earthquakes.

Getting inside volcanoes

I love working on old volcanoes that have been cut into by rivers and glaciers. You can see inside these volcanoes and learn how lava rose to the surface through cracks in the volcano. When I am working on old volcanoes, I never forget my field notebook (see page 19), so that I can sketch the rocks I see and draw cartoons of what I think happened during the eruption.

Did you know?

There are many volcanoes on Earth, but the biggest volcano in the solar system is on Mars. This volcano is called Olympus Mons, and it is almost 388 miles (624 kilometers) wide and 16 miles (25 kilometers) high.

Fieldwork is a big part of my job—and I love it! I usually go on two or three big expeditions every year, mostly to Iceland or Chile. I sometimes go to other places, too, such as Japan, Italy, and the United States. Here is what a typical day is like for me.

7:00 a.m.	Wake up, collect water from a nearby spring, and make oatmeal and coffee for breakfast with my volcanologist friends
8:30 a.m.	Put my boots on (after first emptying all the ash that might have fallen in the day before!) and walk for a couple of hours to an advancing lava flow
10:30 a.m	Arrive at the lava flow and take photographs and measurements
1:00 p.m.	Have lunch next to the lava (but not too close!)

We eat breakfast at our campsite at Cordón Caulle.

1:30 p.m.	Hike to some interesting ash deposits
2:00 p.m.	Take samples of ash
5:00 p.m.	Walk back to the campsite
6:30 p.m.	Arrive at camp and cook a huge meal for everyone
8:00 p.m.	Discuss discoveries with other volcanologists, watch the eruption from our campsite, and look at the stars once night has fallen
10:00 p.m.	Head to my tent and sleep like a log

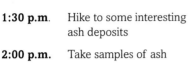

NOTE TO SELF

Don't forget: tent, sleeping bag, camping stove, hammer, sample bags, warm clothes, goggles, sunglasses, first-aid kit, rope, tarp, flashlight, sunblock, camera, solar panel, notebook, several liters of drinking water if needed, rice, vegetables, canned fish, nuts, dried fruit, chocolate. Luxury items: MP3 player, book, candy!

We prepare the evening meal by flashlight.

Our team climbs the ash-covered slope of Cordón Caulle.

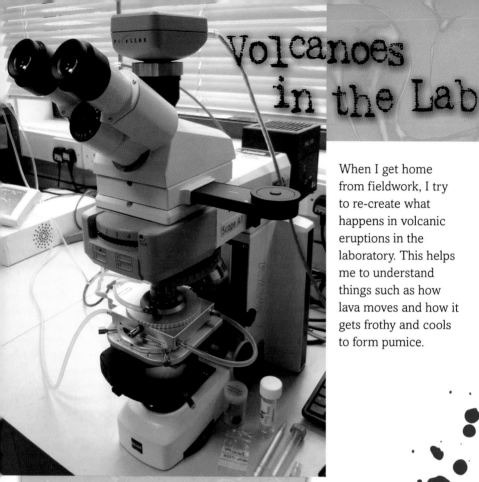

Volcanoes in the Lab

When I get home from fieldwork, I try to re-create what happens in volcanic eruptions in the laboratory. This helps me to understand things such as how lava moves and how it gets frothy and cools to form pumice.

In my lab, I have a special furnace that allows me to cook lava and film what happens through a powerful microscope. I use this to study how crystals and bubbles grow in lava.

Laboratory equipment

We need special equipment to do our experiments. We need furnaces that can reach about 2,750 degrees Fahrenheit (1,500 degrees Celsius) and microphones that we use to record the sound waves made when we smash rocks.

Toasting lava

I also have two pieces of equipment that look a little like toasters! I use these to heat up lava and dry it out. I capture and measure the gases, such as water vapor and carbon dioxide, that are given off as the lava dries out. This helps me to understand a lot about the gases that move inside volcanoes.

This is lava, seen through the microscope. These pictures are less than 1 millimeter across. As the hot lava (top left) cools, crystals form (bottom right), and we can measure how quickly they grow.

RECIPE FOR PUMICE

You need: a pea-sized chunk of lava, sandpaper, a furnace.

1. Collect a piece of lava from a volcano in Iceland.

2. Hand polish the lava until it is no thicker than a piece of paper.

3. Place a tiny piece in the furnace.

4. Heat to 1,562 °F (850 °C) for 5 minutes.

5. Cool quickly and serve!

Detecting chemicals

Understanding what lava and ash are made of is really important. Volcanologists think that gases trapped inside lava, especially water vapor and carbon dioxide, are what creates the pressure that makes volcanoes go BANG!

I work with students at Lancaster University, and many of them are involved in measuring the gases in volcanic rocks. They use amazing equipment to test ideas about what controls eruptions.

There is a competition between us to get to use the most advanced equipment to measure chemicals, and if you're a lucky winner, you need to make the most of the equipment! When Ellen, Jacqui, and I got the chance to shine a very powerful light beam through our lava samples to measure chemicals, we worked in shifts around the clock for four days and collected thousands of measurements.

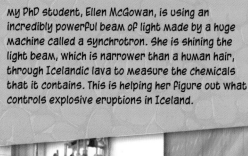

My PhD student, Ellen McGowan, is using an incredibly powerful beam of light made by a huge machine called a synchrotron. She is shining the light beam, which is narrower than a human hair, through Icelandic lava to measure the chemicals that it contains. This is helping her figure out what controls explosive eruptions in Iceland.

This is the equipment that I have used to smash rocks. It is safely housed in an underground lab in London, England.

Rock-breaking work

Finding out how rocks break apart is also really important in understanding volcanoes. Eruptions start when cracks form in the rocks inside volcanoes and lava starts to rise through these cracks to the surface. We are trying to figure out how much pressure is needed for rocks to break, and how this links to the earthquakes that occur just before rocks break. Some of my students break lava in the lab using special, hand-built equipment found nowhere else in the world.

TOOLS OF THE TRADE: HIGH TEMPERATURE TRIAXIAL PRESS

We use a piece of equipment called a high-temperature triaxial press. It has a metal rod called a piston that can put 27.5 tons (25 tonnes) of pressure onto a piece of rock the size of your thumb. This is equal to having 3.5 elephants standing on your thumb! This all happens inside a furnace that goes up to about 1,850 degrees Fahrenheit (1,000 degrees Celsius).

Pouring lava!

It is fun and interesting to work with real lava at incredibly high temperatures. But we have to be very careful – it can also be dangerous. At Syracuse University in the United States, some volcanologists have made amazing lava flows. They melt a huge amount of lava in an outdoor furnace and pour it onto sand and ice. They film the lava up close and measure its temperature. It must be exciting to make a lava flow at the touch of a button!

Did you know?

Hot lava is strange stuff. It doesn't know if it is a solid or a liquid. If you squeeze it slowly, it oozes like thick, hot toothpaste. But squeeze it very quickly and it will shatter like glass. Lava can both shatter and flow inside volcanoes, sometimes at the same time.

These children are toasting marshmallows on the lava made at Syracuse University, in New York!

Sweet-tasting lava!

In our experiments, it can sometimes be safer and easier to use something in place of lava. It needs to be thick and gooey and to move like lava does. One of our favorite things to use is golden syrup, which is similar to molasses. It is the correct thickness and gooeyness, and it behaves a little like runny lava. Some of my colleagues have used enormous tanks of it to examine how lava flows and how bubbles move through it. I wish I could have put some of it on my fieldwork oatmeal!

Comedian Ed Byrne helped volcanologists send bubbles through a tube of golden syrup during a television program about volcanoes in 2012.

A Day in the Office

There is a huge contrast between the work I do in the office and fieldwork. In the office, I have a shorter working day, so that I can spend time with my children. When I am doing fieldwork, the working days can be really long and the expeditions can take weeks. My children will not be joining me on my fieldwork trips until they are in their teens!

6:45 a.m.	Wake up, prepare breakfast
8:15 a.m.	Ride bike to the college nursery, where I drop off my children
9:00 a.m.	Read e-mails and latest volcano news
10:00 a.m.	Go to lab and start new lava cooking experiment
10:45 a.m.	Coffee with the volcanology team
11:30 a.m.	Meet with a student and discuss project on Icelandic volcanoes
12:30 p.m.	Lunch

1:30 p.m.	Write up some results about an eruption in Chile; have a new idea; talk on Skype with a colleague in Germany
4:00 p.m.	Back to lab and check experiment, record results
4:45 p.m.	Pick up children from nursery, ride bike home

5:30–8:00 p.m.
Spend time with my family

8:00–10:00 p.m.
Play cello with my band, rehearsing for a concert

NOTE TO SELF

Many people across the world are interested in volcanoes — especially erupting ones. Another part of my job is to talk about volcanoes — on TV, radio, and for magazines and newspapers. At first, speaking live on radio to many thousands of people was nerve-wracking. But now I really love the chance to share my enthusiasm with other people. I always remind myself to practice how to pronounce some tricky volcano names, such as Eyjafjallajökull, Sakurajima, and Popocatepetl!

How to Become a Volcanologist

Being a volcanologist is a cool job! But you have to be prepared to study and train to do the job. Math, physics, chemistry, geography, and geology are all really useful subjects for future volcanologists.

Higher education

You need to get a college degree in order to become a volcanologist. You could choose to get a degree in geology, geography, environmental science, physics, or chemistry. But that's not all! You also need to get a higher degree, called a master's, in volcanology.

Putting in the hours

After getting a master's degree in volcanology, you could perhaps volunteer to work for free at a volcano observatory or with a volcano research team. This will give you great experience and will help you get a paid job.

Some people also go on to get a PhD. They spend three or four years (or longer!) researching a particular subject in volcanology. Eventually, the aim is to get a great job—doing what you love, while being paid!

TOOLS OF THE TRADE: HIKING BOOTS

A good pair of hiking boots is essential if you want to spend some time climbing on volcanoes. Sometimes I have gone through two pairs in one year! However, you won't be spending all your time outdoors. Much of your work as a volcanologist is spent in the lab and on the computer. So make sure you enjoy desk work, too.

Volcanology students enjoy some spectacular eruptions on Mount Etna, in Italy.

Quiz

Try this quiz to see if you have what it takes to become a volcanologist!

1. On a beach, which of these things would you like to do best?

a) Lie in the sun and read your book

b) Play beach games and go swimming

c) Look through the sand and cliffs for interesting stones and rocks

2. If your sleep is interrupted...

a) You just can't get back to sleep at all and are really tired the next day

b) Nothing can wake you up—you are such a deep sleeper

c) You don't mind—you will just go back to sleep again

3. What would be your ideal workplace?

a) A busy office with lots of people coming and going, where you do the same things every day

b) A factory or workshop where you can make things with your hands

c) A laboratory where you can do experiments

4. If someone asked you to walk far, then up a mountain, carrying a large, heavy backpack...

a) You would say no

b) You would do it, but would moan and groan all the way

c) You wouldn't mind—you like to stay in shape anyway

5. How do you feel about studying hard and taking difficult tests?

a) I'd rather not!

b) I prefer to make things rather than study things

c) I don't mind learning about things that really interest me, and I am prepared to study hard for tests

If you answered mostly Cs, you just might have what it takes to begin exploring a career as a volcanologist!

Glossary

active describes a volcano that has erupted at least once during the last 10,000 years

archaeologist scientist who studies past human lives, especially by examining objects such as pottery, tools, and buildings

ash tiny fragments of jagged rock, minerals, and volcanic glass that look like soft, gray, powdery dust

composition way in which a whole or mixture is made up

computer model program run on a computer that simulates what might happen in real life

crater bowl-shaped opening at the top of a volcano

dike large slab of rock that cuts through another type of rock

element one of the 107 basic substances that can combine with other substances to make other things; for example, water is made of hydrogen combined with oxygen

extinct describes a volcano that has not erupted for at least 10,000 years and is not expected to erupt again

forecast predict

furnace an enclosed structure, like an oven, in which materials are heated to very high temperatures

geology study of the structure of Earth and how it has changed over time; geologists study rocks to find this out

GPS (Global Positioning System) system that uses satellites to pinpoint an exact location on Earth's surface

lava hot, melted rock that erupts from inside a volcano or along a crack in the ground

magma hot, molten rock that rises within volcanoes

monitor study something in order to keep a check on it to see if it changes

PhD often called a doctorate, it is based on at least three years of study on top of a normal college degree and is the highest degree awarded

physics science that looks at matter and energy and how they are related; it includes the study of light, heat, sound, electricity, and force

plain large, flat area of land

plume cloud of gas and fine particles

pressure amount of force upon a surface

pumice lava that has hardened to form a light, porous rock, a bit like a hard sponge

pyroclastic flow flow of volcanic ash, dust, rocks, and debris that rushes down the slope of a volcano during an eruption; they are very dangerous, reaching enormous speeds and temperatures

solar system system that includes a star and all of the things that orbit it, including planets and their moons

thesis very long essay based on research or study, which students write as part of an advanced academic degree

toxic poisonous

tsunami very large sea wave caused by an undersea earthquake or volcanic eruption; these can cause lots of destruction when they hit land

Find Out More

Books

Gazlay, Suzy. *Be a Volcanologist* (Scienceworks!). Pleasantville, N.Y.: Gareth Stevens, 2008.

Hawkins, John. *Volcano Disasters* (Catastrophe!). New York: Rosen Central, 2012.

Mason, Paul. *Into the Fire: Volcanologists* (Scientists at Work). Chicago: Heinemann Library, 2008.

Owen, Ruth. *Volcanologists and Seismologists* (Out of the Lab: Extreme Jobs in Science). New York: PowerKids, 2014.

Web sites

www.bbc.co.uk/programmes/p00v4wkb

You can see a short film I made about the erupting volcano Puyehue in Chile and other short clips all about volcanoes.

kids.discovery.com/games/build-play/volcano-explorer

This fun web site allows you to create your own volcano and watch it erupt.

video.nationalgeographic.com/video/environment/ environment-natural-disasters/volcanoes/ volcanoes-101/

This National Geographic video gives basic information about volcanoes.

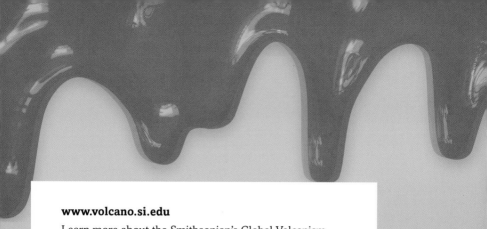

www.volcano.si.edu

Learn more about the Smithsonian's Global Volcanism Program, which works to help people better understand volcanoes and volcanic activity.

volcanoes.usgs.gov

On this web site, there is a huge amount of information, games, videos, and photos.

Topic for research

There is a lot you can learn before you decide to become a volcanologist. Go to your local library and find all the books you can on volcanoes. Read them and try to understand as much as you can about them. Look out for any news stories about volcanoes around the world and find out what volcanologists are doing in these places.

Index

active volcanoes 10, 17, 44
ancient volcanoes 28, 29
ash 5, 6, 13, 15, 16, 17, 21, 26, 27, 28, 30, 31, 34, 44
avalanches 16

camping 8, 11, 12, 27, 30, 31
college classes 7, 8, 40
computer modeling 4, 14, 23, 44
Cordón Caulle 5, 18, 26, 27, 30, 31
craters 12, 17, 27, 44

deaths 12, 13, 14

earthquakes 9, 11, 14, 17, 29, 35
eruptions 5, 7, 8, 9, 12, 13, 14, 15, 17, 18, 19, 20, 21, 26, 28, 31, 35
evacuation 13, 17, 20
explosive eruptions 18, 26
extinct volcanoes 6, 7, 44
Eyjafjallajökull 15, 17

fieldwork 8–9, 24–27, 30–31, 38
floods 16, 19, 21
forecasting 5, 14, 17, 20, 44
furnaces 32, 35, 36

gases 13, 14, 17, 22, 27, 33, 34
geologists 23
GPS (Global Positioning System) 25, 44
Guðmundsson, Magnús Tumi 23

hazards of volcanoes 16
high-temperature triaxial press 35
hot pools 9
Hrafntinnusker 28

ice-covered volcanoes 16, 19, 21, 23

Katla 21
Kilauea 24

Krakatoa 5

laboratory work 4, 11, 20, 32–35, 38, 39, 41
lava 4, 5, 6, 7, 9, 11, 12, 14, 16, 18, 20, 22, 23, 24, 25, 26, 28, 29, 30, 32, 33, 34, 35, 36–37, 44

magma 18, 44
Mars 29
monitoring volcanoes 13, 16, 17, 44
Mount Etna 7, 20, 24, 25, 41
Mount St. Helens 12
Mount Unzen 13
Mount Vesuvius 14, 15

notebooks 19, 29

office work 38–39, 41
Olympus Mons 29

permeameters 23
physicists 23
protective clothing 25
pumice 4, 15, 27, 32, 33, 45
pyroclastic flows 13, 14, 15, 27, 45

safety 5, 25, 27
samples, collecting 9, 25, 26

Taupo 10
teamwork 22–23
thunderstorms 18
Torfajökull 8–9
toxic metals 22
tsunamis 16, 45

volcanic rocks 23, 35
Volvan Osorno 19

working day 30–33, 38–39